POEMS

by

James Troy Turner

CLADACH
Publishing

An AGATES Book of Poetry

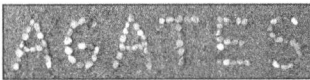

Published by
CLADACH Publishing
PO Box 336144
Greeley, CO 80633
http://cladach.com

The editorial assistance of Peggi Fulton is gratefully
acknowledged.

Library of Congress Control Number: 2016913711

ISBN-13: 9780989101462
ISBN-10: 0989101460

Second printing
Printed in the U.S.A.

James Troy Turner today…

…and as a young man

PREFACE

James Troy Turner (Troy) has been writing poetry for many years. The original poems published herein were written on napkins, on the pages of notebooks, journals, and legal pads, to name a few—whatever paper Troy had handy when inspiration came.

Through the years he saved his verse, finally deciding to bring it to publication.

Troy's nephew, John Turner, has this to say about Troy as a poet:

> "All great writers have one thing in common: the real life experiences it takes to be one. Troy Turner has a knack for bringing this worldliness, and the thoughts and feelings that go with it, from being trapped in memory to ink on paper—with true expression."

Be prepared to enjoy looking at the depths of Troy's heart and beliefs through these honest, heartfelt poems, inspired by the Word of God and by Troy's life.

CONTENTS

Friends

Stay beside me as time goes by.
I call you friend; I'll tell you why.
Through thick and thin, it stays the same;
To break these ties would be a shame.

Though people come and people go,
A friend is someone you always know.
Depend on me as I do you,
Whatever the task, we'll make it through.

Judgment

When we judge each other
  we see only one way;
To look at one's self
  cannot happen today.
"Oh, that's what's wrong,"
  we say to another.
He says, "That's right,
  look at yourself, brother."

God

I kneel before You on bended knees,
  praying for forgiveness
For all the evils I have done
  to which You are the witness.

It comes to me to come to You.
  Your open arms wait patient.
The sins were trapped within my soul;
  I was an evil servant.

You cleansed my soul and healed me up
  with tender love and care.
I only wish that I had known
  that You were always there.

And now You live within my heart,
  all fibers of my being.
In You faith soars in highest flight,
  and evil is sent fleeing.

Quarrel Solitude

This poem I write with
  open heart, open mind,
To open the door to love
  closed up inside.

I loved you long ago;
  it was good even though
hard times began.
  Now I love you again;
  but I think not as much
  as tomorrow.
Love should not bring
  so much sorrow.

What must I do
  to bring us into today,
Only leaving our yesterday
  for a bright tomorrow.

Burning Flag

The President said
   we have no right;
Our Constitution says
   we do.
"To burn our flag
   is desecration."
I think that it
   is up to you.
To alter our rights
   would be a sin,
To take away
   our freedom.
Will history tell
   a sad, sad story,
Or will freedom
   win again?

Fade to Black

Open spaces in our lives
   are closing in on me
With open arms of endless fate
   and rapture left unseen.
The walls of life, the grip of death,
   and hopes and dreams unseen.

The wonders of a million things
   are we the chosen ones.
We walk, we talk, we sing
   of life and all of our life's joys.
We cry, we shout, we run about
   as if we are God's toys.

When we are gone no song is sung,
   no laughter can be heard.
We fade to black without a fight,
   without a single word.

Philosophy

To move in a new direction
  is to open the inner self
  to new adventures and goals.

Resolve

Broken inside and making the effort
  takes a lot of pride in pushing forward.
Without reservation, having and holding
  makes it worth the resolution.

Friendship in Return

A friend to me
  can only be
  someone who cares
  from deep inside;
One who is fair
  but not always right,
  and likes what is seen
  with themselves in sight;
One who is true
  and may sometimes
  need help.
When I think back,
  I've been there myself.

Inspiration

Inspired by need,
  driven by desire,
The end draws nearer
  hour by hour.

Struggles in life
  bring pain and dismay.
Stop—look around;
  now you must pray.

The tools for salvation
  are close at hand.
Through rapture and grace
  come promised land.

A Sea of Emotion

Lost in a sea of emotion,
  no one to help me,
  no one to love.

12-oz cans don't
  turn you away;
And if they do, you
  don't need them anyway.

My heart is swollen,
  my head's in a spin;
When it comes to love,
  where do you begin?

I have a heart—
  I want to love, be loved.
I'd almost sell my soul for love.
  But do I have a soul?

The sea covers me.

Love for Love

Why do I do this to myself,
  you may ask.
But do you know the
  requirements of the task?

To give themselves
  without any meaning
Is the life others live,
  without ever feeling.

To have and to hold
  for the rest of my life
Is the most I desire,
  the point of my strife.

My Family

A family is wholesome,
   so solid and true;
You can talk to them
   when nothing to do.

You pour out your heart
   and tell them the least;
And never regret
   your having the least.

Your sister and brother
   do mean such a lot;
But they can't replace
   the love you have not.

Looking Into You

Look into the still, cool stream,
  mind wandering, wandering, wandering.
Look into your rambling soul.
  My friend, where will the venture
  bring your conscious mind?—
Deep into the dark pit
  of subconscious meditation
  till you stand freely,
  unmoving, unfeeling, unknowing.
You may stay in this world of the dead
  if you wish,
  willing never to return.
Lonely, sad souls live there waiting
  to show you the way.
  But don't stay.
Go to the sun instead: shining, gleaming,
  showing the way to others
  who stand with you at their side.

Wedge of Satan

Misunderstanding is the pulpit of evil.
It eats through your soul as the grain with the weevil.
Your ears standing up and listening so strong,
It's hard to believe there's a chance you heard wrong.
Let God listen for you; He'll show you the way.
Live happy and cherish each God-given day.

Thoughts of Eve

I think of Eve both night and day,
  with the song of love unborn;
And when my soul begins to sing,
  I want her more and more.

To touch and hold and comfort now,
  to keep and be with forever.
What the hell am I writing this for;
  Her love will blossom never.

Oh, now is my heart broken apart,
  never to mend in the future.
Oh, what can I do with not even a clue.
  There must be a gentle Teacher.

My pencil runs wild with words compiled
  that make no sense or reason.
What can I do, my brain's in a stew;
  It must be the changing season.

So late at night I've put up a fight
  to sleep, but it's only depressing.
I'll lay down my pen and try it again;
  But it seems like I'm only regressing.

Oh, Eve, come to me, I plead with thee;
  I love your ways and your style.
It happens to be all that I can see;
  In my dreams is only your smile.

Snowflakes

I watch the snowflakes as they fall;
They hit the ground and fade away,
So soft and gentle as they touch;
So dry, a tear holds twice as much.
Beautiful to see, so fragile to hold,
No tears could ever be so cold.

The End

Deeper and deeper into the open arms of death,
As the world lives, then what time is left.
We push and we pull, filling our lives
With only the promise of tomorrow.
And where is the light?

Lonely is the Man

Lonely is the man with his face in his hands;
Thought is his world, his beloved homeland.
Open your eyes, look into the skies
As autumn leaves fall from the trees,
And the song of his heart is a fading beat.
Lonely is this space so full of empty ambition,
Working so hard with no rhyme or reason.
Look into your soul, open your heart;
There is beauty in the depths of this season.

The Poet

I want to be published
  to earn notoriety,
And to say the least,
  give my life variety.
To make it big
  in the world of linguists.
The only trouble is
  I caint hardly speak English.

Forgiven

These days are so hard—
  the nights are so long.
Do I stay up at night
  to hear sweet angel song?
Life plays such mean tricks
  on you day after day;
All night I stay up
  and I pray and I pray.
Life's ends are all raveled
  and my thoughts so unreal,
And satan's just out there,
  our souls he would steal.
God scratches His circle
  in indelible ink,
Our souls safe inside it;
  God's Son we must thank.

The Plan

My sins have gone before me,
  my soul is at peace now.
God gave His only Son for this,
  and it makes me weep so now.
God spread His seed on mother earth
  so with fruit and grain she'd abound;
Then man came along behind Him
  and walked on the sacred ground
And ate the fruit from the sacred tree
  around which satan had wound.
The wrath of God through His divine curse,
  the earth once more sat on solid ground.
The works of God that Jesus bore,
  His Son, so weak and earthy;
The trouble I'm not sure about—
  that man is even worthy.

Disaster

Now it comes clear
　　just as before,
With arms closed tight
　　and through the night
　　loving rapture tore.

　　It's not so.

In from the dark
　　without uttering a word,
Our hearts torn apart
　　by what satan has heard.
He's come to bear ill
　　against you and me.
He heard of a weakness
　　not easy to see.

　　Fill me in.

With God's loving help,
　　it's easy to see,
I'd rather be dead,
　　laid under a tree.
With Your holy grace
　　is where I should be.

Eternity

I vow I shall fight
  by the side of the Lord,
To help Him in wielding
   His double-edged sword.

Our victory is satan's
  demise, there's no doubt.
God's kingdom shall reign
  till time has run out.

Dreams

I want you, you want me;
we want only what we see
when we're asleep at night.

His Word

My Father is coming for me,
  I hear.
The angels all singing in glee,
  no fear.
Whatever will be will be,
  so near.
The angels all running,
  so free.

The Word is delivered to me,
  I hear.
The Bible's not sent to deceive,
  no fear.
Deception's beginning its reap,
  so near.
So what have they all got to fear?—
  NOT ME.

Deception

I don't know if I can forget how it felt
  when my sweetheart said to me
Her spiritual life had been shaded with strife
  the last seven months with me.

And now I look into myself
  to see what I can see,
But there is nothing to lighten my soul.
  How has it been taken from me?

All the Really Good Poems
Never Get Written

How does it come to me; it's so clear,
   the struggle with writing it right.
The words all arranged a particular way,
   the words walk me through the night.

It's not I who does this,
   but instead it is told
A well-trained pen scribbles
   its words so bold.
And I just sleep all the night away.

Don't let it fool you, I work like a fool;
   yet the sun starts another day.

Home

Lighten your heart,
  unfetter your soul.
To live with our Lord
  is our spiritual goal.
Open your eyes
  to His holiest Word.
It's righteous salvation
  your soul overheard.
Come dream a sweet dream,
  come hear the sweet song.
My soul goes to God,
  that's where it belongs.

Through Crimson Canyons

Through crimson canyons,
  hearts so bold,
We ride our horses
  as life unfolds,
To reach each other,
  soul held out,
To find another
  we can care about;
To bind our thoughts,
  to share our strife,
To be part of
  each others' lives.
In crimson canyons
  our fate is blessed,
To life and love—
  we concede the rest.

I Want to be Free

I want to be free
  to run through the trees,
  to fly where the eagle dares.

To walk through the flowers
  or idle away hours,
  or discover a new thought to share.

With love in my heart
  when holding you tight;
  the joy of knowing you care.

Walking on the beach
  or hearing a speech,
  or just spending time with you.

It doesn't take much
  to be free as a breeze;
If there's always you and me,
  our dreams can stay free.

Time

The last two weeks with you
  are wondrous in their way,
Though strife and struggle seem
  to hinder in many ways.
From now till eternity
  I love you through every day.
Through webs of delusion and fear,
  my faith grows stronger each day.

Thought

Sitting here just passing time,
Expressing feelings that I'm glad are mine.
Think of a subject, then jot it down,
Then think of another, and mull it around.

I'm really not a poet;
If you read this, then you'll know it.
But I have fun trying—
To stop would be like dying.

Wages of Sin

Wages of sin
  is all man's device
To comfort
  and embellish his flesh.
Just live and die
  with God in your life
Or tag along
  with the rest.
Open your mind
  and you might realize
That comfort and gold
  are His test.

Rapture

God take me from bondage
  in this life, I pray.
Life seems to get harder
  each day after day.
By Your side I am destined
  to fight on that day
When Jesus comes riding
  all evil to slay.
God take me to Your kingdom,
  Your Word to protect,
For satan's right behind You
  with his waiting bondage net.

Nam Vet

The unsung hero has nowhere to go,
  nothing to see and nothing to show.
Back from the fight with the other side,
  thinking how lucky just to be left alive.
Lonely and forgotten, without even a clue,
  remembering how easily he had been used.

Water runs deep, they say, under the bridge,
  through hills and towns and over the ridge.
"Run through me, river of blood," he demands.
  "Give life to these limbs, I must make a stand.
Give me my life and leave me my soul."
  To just stay alive is his life-long goal.

Unknown Poet

The unknown poet strikes again
  in fun with words that rhyme,
The meanings of which are misconstrued
  and altered from time to time.

The point is blunt with meaning up front,
  but between the lines are read:
Nobody can make it in this world
  until we all are dead.

I hope this verse will live beyond
  the borders of my time.
For writing it I know that I
  will never get a dime.

Riches

Heir to nothing,
  my will still holds strong.
My morals are good,
  tho' I know not how long.
My life lies before me;
  what path will I take?
My memories help guide me,
  the truth in their wake.

Ramblings of a Madman

I'm here today and gone tomorrow;
  but in their souls there is no sorrow.
The torch is lit, no time to borrow;
  for you'll awake and there'll be no tomorrow.
So live your life, forget the sorrow,
  and forget the days and forget the morrow.
Forget the strife that it takes to survive,
  and forget to thank God that you are alive.
Remember the good times, they'll not happen again;
  Remember me always, I'm really your friend.

On Top of the World

You know what happens;
  the way it goes,
  the way it comes out
  no one knows.
The Word of God seems
  to stand me up;
  satan tries to
  drain my cup.
The world goes round,
  seems to never stop;
  the world goes round
  and round and round.
It spins so fast
  without a sound;
  but I stand up tall,
  I feel on top.
God's strength and love,
  so real and true—
  if you let it—
  will grow in you.

Season of Time

As the seasons pass
  I can't help but wonder;
The antichrist comes,
  God's wing we're under.
As time flies by,
  our lives asunder,
Let time and seasons
  come together.
Our faith in God
  time must weather;
As seasons and signs
  pass by, let's gather.

The Rapture

Once again it comes to pass,
  our Lord and Savior comes at last
Preceded by the evil one,
  a life of anguished strife for some.
On big white horses both will ride;
  so stand with God's Word by your side.

Don't fly away upon first sight;
  for that would be to satan's delight.
To witness for Jesus is the only way
  when antichrist tries your faith to sway.
And then you'll be with the holy one,
  as life eternal goes on and on!

Pass to Heaven

Another look at life's little pleasures,
   the ups and downs so easy to weather,
The ins and outs, there's so little doubt
   that pain and misfortune you can't live without.

With love and friendship you never go wrong,
   a companion and partner your whole life long.
Someone to depend on through bliss and strife,
   to share all the aspects of your passing life.

A walk on the beach, a ride in a car,
   or stopping to think, just right where you are.
The pleasures of life abound every day;
   get out there and ride the rollercoaster today.

To live in God is so easy and right;
   with forgiveness of sins, Jesus had us in sight.
The gift is so grand, God's Son knew His plight.
   A free pass to heaven, His Word shows the way:
   Just walk the righteous path of God every day.

Clay Pot

The urn of life so lightly broken,
Closer to God now the end is spoken.
The goals in life so clear when you're young,
The songs of happiness left unsung.
Still holding on to righteous faith,
There's happiness still in my wake.

Remember it all has not gone wrong;
Stand up strong, sing proud my song.
The love of God is important to me.
Whatever His plan will be, will be.
Open your eyes and you will see
My soul next to God my future to be.

Forgiveness

Facts of life
  rap on the door,
A life lived hard
  like that of a whore.
The blood of Christ
  will wash over you.
Life everlasting
  you will start anew.
The promise was made
  a long time ago,
Never forgotten;
  you know it is so.

Deceived

Inwardly I fly to the
center of my conscious hope.
My determined goals dangle
at the end of a limp rope.
The thrust of lonely ambition
works hard in my very being.
The results are well hidden,
to the blind are left unseen.
I'm learning to fly! In
joyous hope I wildly swing.
Anxiety and wonder abound,
and my soul joyously sings.
The wonders of life
are often left unknown;
but make a mistake
and you could break a bone.
If you unknowingly follow satan,
this is the way it will be.
But wait and witness for Jesus;
just follow the free.
"Don't be deceived,"
the Word of God says.
Don't step on a rake,
you'll only break your head!

Youth

What happened to my childhood,
  days I thought would never end.
My mind is full of the memories
  which seem to have no end.
Cut short by all that happened,
  all of life that has happened since,
The good and the bad—
  mostly not worth two cents.
As young and as free
  as the air and the trees;
As light and carefree
  as a scent in the breeze.
Those days have come and gone;
  all I can do is remember.
Now as I have lived,
  my time is in December.
Thank God it hasn't been wasted;
  it all had great meaning.
I survived all my childhood
  and now feel that I'm winning.

Stuff

My poems aren't long and fancy;
  they're made of what I feel.
And when you hear or read them,
  you know that they are real.

Inspired by events that pass
  as with the sands of time;
Not by the pieces of sand
  that end up in your eyes.

A blessing from the Lord,
  I thank Him every day.
But inspiration leaves me—
  sometimes it fades away.

I ask myself is it long enough,
  I really rack my mind
To sort out all the stuff;
  before I know just what to do,
  my silly poem is through.

Truth

How I long for the days of
  My simple youth.
You could believe all they said—
  You knew it was true.
A man was a man always,
  True even to himself.
The goods he would buy—
  Top quality on each shelf.
But those days are past,
  I think never to be again.
Listen hard what they say—
  Truth and lies in a spin.

Abomination

Destroyed in His wrath
  in the past,
Sodom and Gomorrah
  cannot last.
They have taken my rights
  and discarded my life.
I don't want to live in this
  corruption and strife.
I'm unable to work with
  this dysfunctional life.
It has come to pass,
  but I hope it doesn't last.
My Savior, come back—
  I hope fast.

Worldly

I am so far off the bubble
sitting idle in all this rubble.
It really doesn't make any sense;
my understanding has long been spent.
Reality is left so unraveled,
no common sense, and now I'm baffled.
I live by His Word, you know it's true:
Followers of satan are all but through.
It all adds up to endless trouble;
The wrath of God, it will be double.
So trust in Him, His will be done.
And if you do, you're loved like His son.

I John 2:16

Block Head

I have a block inside my head;
It seems like inspiration is dead.
I push the words in and out of my mind;
But the results of this are not too kind.
Through restless nights and eventless days,
I hope that life will change those ways.
As days go by my faith stays strong;
But the way things go, I don't know how long.

What Word?

I feel like an anchor
  dropped without its rope.
In what I say, the meaning's
  left without a hope.
Given a true task,
  I studied without end.
At completion of my study
  the answer I would send.
The answer book's not written
  with the answer stashed inside
For the work that I have done,
  with result that's not alive.
The Bible says don't give up,
  until the answer's found.
But the work I've done
  in that respect
  has been buried underground.

Bureaucrats

They wait till you're down
Then they kick you around.
Their eyes see no more than their noses.

Their lives have been easy;
By living so sleazy
They always come out smelling like roses.

You know what I'm saying?
They all should be praying.
They'll die, not just pushing up posies.

Was & Is

I was a young man then, so wild and so free,
My goals set high, my soul above the trees.
I've heard it said, "If I'd only known then."
But if we had known, where would it begin?

Like I say, we may have fallen in the beginning;
But when we start running is when we start winning.

ABOUT THE POET

James Troy Turner was born in 1949 to parents who moved state to state following the harvest of various fruits. When he was four years old, Troy's parents divorced. After attending many schools and doing poorly with his studies, Troy transferred to Woodlin High School in northeast Colorado. While he was at Woodlin, Troy had an inspiring English teacher, Ethel Dean Bell, whom he credits with instilling in him the desire to write. He graduated in 1969. That same year Troy received a draft notice. He joined the U.S. Navy and served in the Mediterranean on the USS Canisteo during the Vietnam War.

After being honorably discharged from the Navy, Troy attended Denver Automotive and Diesel College and graduated in 1972. He has been married and divorced three times.

These are some comments his friends have made about Troy:

"Troy is an observant man of depth with a desire for truth, love for his God, and growing gentleness."

"Troy is a straight shooter and a pillar to his friends."

"Troy is very kindhearted."

As for himself, Troy humbly professes he appreciates life and loves God and Jesus.

He lives in Colorado.

www.ingramcontent.com/pod-product-compliance
Lightning Source LLC
Chambersburg PA
CBHW031600040426
42452CB00006B/361